MW01533370

LIVING FOR CHRIST AT HOME

An Encouragement for Teens

LISSY BAILEY

TABLE OF CONTENTS

LET'S GET STARTED

How do we as teenagers, live for Christ at home with our families? If you are growing up in a Christian church, you have probably heard messages like, "Be a light in your community! Reach your friends for Christ! Show Christ's love to others!"

While all of this is true and important, I believe that we frequently neglect to practice these things within our homes and with our families. The home is where our true character is revealed and the sad truth is that our families often get the worst of our personalities. Think of it this way. When was the last time you stormed out of a classroom after yelling at your teacher? The answer for many of us would be never. However, when was the last time you yelled or got annoyed at a parent or sibling?

Living for Christ goes so much deeper than just being a "good person" at school or church. One of the greatest tests of spiritual maturity is our attitude and actions towards our own family. **Who we are at home is who we really are.** Let that sink in for a second. I know for me, it doesn't take long to see that my character at home needs some serious improvement.

I will be the first to admit that living for Christ at home is a struggle! As a natural extrovert, I tend to give my energy and passion to things outside my home without thinking of how God might use me to minister and bless my family.

It is easy to *talk* about being a Christian with your family but what steps can we take today to *live* it out? In this study, we will look at four biblical virtues—honor, love, honesty, and service. We will talk about the challenge and power of living out these virtues at home.

Every family is different and has unique challenges. Some of us have Christian parents, others do not. Some of us live with only one of our parents. Regardless of your family situation, God can use the virtues that we will discuss to make an impact in your life, faith, and family.

HONOR

As I mentioned before, one of the greatest tests of our spiritual maturity is our attitude and actions at home. Perhaps one of the hardest relationships that every teen faces is the relationship with their parents. The fifth commandment says, *"Honor your father and your mother, that your days may be long in the land that the Lord your God is giving you"* (Exodus 20:12).

Many of us are familiar with this commandment and it is easy to dismiss its significance. For a long time, I thought that this command simply meant, "obey your parents." In general, I try to obey my parents when they tell me to do something. Often I would think to myself, "All right, I'm an obedient kid, I think I have this commandment down. However, a couple years ago, God convicted me of the true meaning of the fifth commandment.

In Ephesians 6, we are told not simply to obey our parents, but to honor them. The word honor is a verb and defined as, "to hold in honor or high respect; revere" (Dictionary.com). Do I hold my parents in honor and high respect? Sure, I was obedient (for the most part) but was that really honoring them? It is possible to have obedience with a dishonoring heart behind it.

For example, if my parents asked me to clean my room (which they often do), and I obey—yet complain and grumble the whole time—did I honor them? I obeyed, but my heart was in the wrong place. That's not honor! Honor combines both action and attitude.

Truly honoring your parents goes deeper than just obedience. We must pray and ask God to give us a heart of service and reverence towards our parents.

As you will see in the Scripture below, we are called to obey and honor our parents *in the Lord.* This means that we are not required to obey our parents if they tell us to do something that God says is wrong. Also, if our parents are acting in ways that are hurtful to us we should reach out for help.

The commandment to honor our parents is a lifelong challenge. While we may not have to obey our parents when we become adults, the call to honor them will be present our whole lives. Why not start practicing this life-long command now, so that we may be prepared for the future?

None of this is easy! I will be the first to acknowledge that this is very difficult and my headstrong nature often falls prey to dishonor, especially when I am at home. Yet God does not leave us to struggle alone and gives us the strength we need each and every day.

In these moments, I've found that a quick prayer can help turn my heart to the mission of honoring my parents.

> *"Lord, help me to honor and serve my parents today. Please give me a heart of service and respect towards them even when it is difficult. I cannot do this alone and I need your help to change the attitude of my heart towards my parents. Amen."*

Scripture and Questions for Reflection/Discussion:

Children, obey your parents in the Lord, for this is
right. "Honor your father and mother" (this is the first
commandment with a promise), "that it may go well
with you and that you may live long in the land." Fathers,
do not provoke your children to anger, but bring them
up in the discipline and instruction of the Lord.

EPHESIANS 6:1–4

1. Do you find it difficult to honor your parents? If so, why is
    honor so challenging?

    Kinda. I feel like I respect them More often how that I'm older to.

2. What are some practical ways that you can honor your
    parents at home? Be specific.

    listen to them, doht argue or grumble, see them as the leaders asa stessexes.

3. To grow in honor, we must first repent of dishonor. Have
    you ever confessed this to the Lord? If not, take time to do
    that now in prayer.

    ok did it :)

4. If you need to ask your parents to forgive you for dishonor,
    pray for God to give you the courage and humility to do it.

    ok.

LOVE

When I was younger, my mom would always say to me, "Your siblings are your best friends. Everyone else will come in and out of your life but your siblings will always be there."

At the time, I quickly dismissed this and thought, "Well, if they are my best friends, they certainly don't act like it." Whenever I would do something rude or hurtful to a sibling, my mom would ask me, "Is that how you would treat your best friend?" The answer was almost always a resounding, "no." The question that followed was, "What if you treated your best friends the way you treat your siblings?" The simplest answer was, "I wouldn't have any friends." Yet as I have gotten older, God has begun to turn my heart to the ministry of my siblings, and I'm beginning to see the incredible blessing they can be in my life.

As I mentioned in the last chapter, living for Christ at home with your family is not as easy as it seems. As teenagers, the world constantly tries to pull our hearts away from the ministry to our families. Perhaps one of the most obvious places this happens is in our relationships with our brothers and sisters. In fact, the stereotype in our culture is that siblings are supposed to hate each other. (With four brothers and two sisters, I'll admit my patience is often tested.)

The prevailing view is that siblings and friends just do not mix together. I know I feel this "battle" going on inside of me—I always seem to want to hang out with my friends and not spend time with my brothers or sisters. While everyone says this is a normal part of adolescence, I think it is a spiritual battle for our God-given relationships with our brothers and sisters.

So where do we start? Forgiveness and prayer.

First, **forgiveness.** For many of us, past hurts can keep us from opening up to our siblings. Learning to forgive, and to forgive often, is a skill that we all need throughout our lives. It's because God chose our siblings as the people that will be closest to us that they also hold some of the greatest power to hurt us. So the first step in (re)building a sibling relationship may involve forgiving a sibling for something they have done or continue to do to you. Or maybe you need to ask a sibling for forgiveness because of ways you have hurt them.

This is not easy! Those hurts can be deep and very painful. Yet holding grudges destroys relationships. I have talked to many adults that have little to no relationships with their siblings due to past hurts or conflicts. Learning to forgive your siblings now can preserve a relationship for the future. However, God is the only one that can give us hearts of true forgiveness towards our siblings. We must ask for His help each and every day.

The second step in prioritizing a sibling relationship is **prayer.** I am 18 years old and my sister Laynie is 13. We have a great relationship now and I value her as one of my best friends in the world. However, our relationship has not always been what it is today. When we were younger, about ages 12 and 8, we were terrible to each other. We shared a room, which in and of it itself presented a multitude of conflicts. I was bossy and insensitive, while she was rude and disrespectful. Any time our mom asked us to clean our room it would typically end with both of us in tears, refusing to speak to each other.

Over the years, I had deeply hurt and been hurt by my younger sister. Our hearts were far from each other and our friendship was in pieces. However, our relationship hit a turning point when our parents encouraged us to pray with one another. It was not easy at first and very awkward, but eventually we got to a point where we would say a prayer together every night before going to bed. If I forgot to pray one night, I would hear her little voice from the top bunk saying, "Lissy, can we pray together?" This small step of prayer brought healing and forgiveness to our relationship in miraculous ways. If you have younger siblings, it is up to you to take the lead and be the first one to offer grace and forgiveness.

Prayer is vital to sibling relationships! We often share prayer requests with our friends but when was the last time you asked your sibling how you could pray for them, or asking them to pray for you?

I think the answer for many of us would be never. I want a relationship with my siblings such that when I have a family of my own, they are the first people I call when I am in need of prayer. I'm guessing many of you want that, too? Yet in order to have that kind of relationship, we need to start the practice of prayer with our siblings while we are still at home!

Lastly, be **intentional** with your siblings! This can be as easy as taking a sister out for coffee or throwing a football with a younger brother. My mom always encouraged us to include our siblings with our friends. I love hanging out with my brothers and we often will hang out together in groups of people. Don't let a busy schedule keep you from spending quality time with your siblings. The relational benefits and friendships are so worth your time. I can honestly say that through spending intentional time with my siblings they have become some of my closest and trusted friends.

I fail so often at treating my siblings like they are my best friends. I can be rude, bossy, and cranky, and they can be equally as difficult. However, I would not trade my God-given relationship with any of them. We cannot love our siblings through our own strength. We must pray and ask God to fill our hearts with forgiveness and love. Often times that prayer can go something like this,

God, please turn my heart towards the ministry to my siblings. Thank you that you have given them to me as my best friends. Please help me forgive them for any ways they have hurt me and please make me aware of ways that I may have hurt them. Please help me to be intentional with them and be filled with gentleness and love. Amen.

Scripture and Questions for Reflection/Discussion:

And you shall love the Lord your God with all your heart and with all your soul and with all your mind and with all your strength.' The second is this: 'You shall love your neighbor as yourself.' There is no other commandment greater than these."

MARK 12:30-31

Bearing with one another and, if one has a complaint against another, forgiving each other; as the Lord has forgiven you, so you also must forgive.

COLOSSIANS 3:13

So if you are offering your gift at the altar and there remember that your brother has something against you, leave your gift there before the altar and go. First be reconciled to your brother, and then come and offer your gift.

MATTHEW 5:23-24

1. How do each of these scriptures apply to your relationship with your sibling?

2. What would it look if you treated your sibling more like your best friend?

3. What are some practical ways you can be intentional with your siblings while also balancing a busy schedule?

4. Write down one small thing you can do to show love to a sibling this week.

HONESTY

Solomon writes to his son in Proverbs 23:26 saying, "My son, give me your heart." For many teenagers this sounds strange. What does it mean to "give our heart" to our parents?

The truth is that one of the most vital pieces of any parent-child relationship is heart connection. Heart connection produces a relationship filled with warmth, openness, honesty, and trust. Your parents want this kind of relationship with you. As teenagers, in many ways we dictate how much of our hearts we choose to share with our parents.

If God calls us to give our hearts to our parents then why is it so difficult to talk to them or tell them what's going on in our lives? Imagine this scenario. I am coming home from youth group and the second I walk in the door my mom says, "How was youth group tonight?" My automatic response is to give the shortest answer possible and avoid a long conversation. This answer is not because I dislike my parents, I am simply giving a default reply without really thinking about it.

The world would say this is a normal part of adolescence and that we should not pursue a close relationship with our parents. I would argue that this is a spiritual attack on our heart connection with our parents.

Your parents are called by God to point you to Christ and therefore they have the most influence over your heart. When we are spiritually connected with our parents, we are better prepared to face attacks against our faith. Our parents can help us grow in our faith and maturity as we venture into adult life. We have a crisis of people in our generation that are turning away from faith in God and His Word. This is not a problem with our church youth groups or children's programs, it is a problem of the family and brokenness in parent-child relationships. This is why the enemy will do everything in his power to keep you from sharing your heart with your parents.

Many of us wish to give our hearts to our parents but the essential question is how? First of all, we must pray and ask God to soften our hearts toward our parents. Then we must start somewhere! Like anything in life, the more you practice sharing your life and being honest with your parents the more it will seem normal and natural. A start could be something as small as giving your parents real answers when they ask questions about your life. Tell them when you feel stressed or anxious. Build the habit of asking your parents to pray for you as well as asking how you can pray for them. Learn to forgive fully and often. One of the most destructive elements of all relationships is holding on to past hurts. It is so easy to harbor a spirit of bitterness towards our parents. We must ask God to give us a heart of forgiveness in order to rebuild heart connection with them.

Perhaps one of the most difficult areas of our lives to share with our parents is romantic relationships. As a girl, I always found it much easier to talk to my mom about relationships than my dad. To be perfectly honest, the idea of telling my dad who I liked or asking him for relationship advice made me feel so awkward. However, a few years ago, God convicted me that I needed to be giving my heart to my dad when it came to relationships. I remember the first time I tried to talk to him about this area of my life I had this horrible pit in my stomach. Yet after we talked and I shared my heart, the sense of love and closeness that I felt towards my dad was overwhelming. To be honest, even after that first conversation, talking to my dad about boys didn't get any easier. For about a year I felt that pit in my stomach before every conversation. But because I started practicing early, now our relationship is at the point where I feel comfortable sharing anything about my life with him especially in regards to boys and relationships.

Looking back, I can see the enemy was trying to keep me from sharing my heart with my dad. Our fathers are our spiritual authority and Satan will do everything in his power to keep our hearts as far away from each other as possible. It is important to be aware of this as we must consciously make an effort to give our hearts to our parents in all areas of our life.

Giving our hearts to our parents is difficult and will meet spiritual resistance. However, my encouragement is to start small and start today! Learning to give your heart to your parents will benefit your relationship with them for the rest of your life. We must continually ask God to soften our hearts towards them. For me, praying something like this throughout the day makes a big difference.

> *Lord, soften my heart towards my parents. Please help me to give them my heart even when it is hard and I don't want to. I pray against any spiritual attack on our relationship and that you would fill my heart with openness and love towards my parents. Amen.*

Scripture and Questions for Reflection/Discussion:

But if we walk in the light, as he is in the light, we
have fellowship with one another, and the blood
of Jesus his Son cleanses us from all sin.

1 JOHN 1:7

My son, give me your heart.

PROVERBS 23:26A

1. How does 1 John 1:7 apply to our heart connection (our fellowship) with our parents?

2. To what degree are you honest with your parents about your personal life? What has been your experience in the past when you have been honest with them about personal things?

3. Is there a particular area of your life that is difficult to share with your parents?

4. We al struggle being open with our parents. Pray and ask God to help you "start somewhere" to share more of your life with your parents (school, friends, relationships, fears etc.)

SERVICE

In our culture and communities, we talk a lot about leadership. How can you be a leader among your friends? How can you be a leader at school? How can you be a leader in the world? Although leadership is a valuable attribute, I believe that we have lost one of the most important aspects of leadership. If we really want to be Christian leaders, we should look to the Bible for our definition.

Jesus lived out what it meant to lead others through service and humility. Mark 10:42–45 says, "And Jesus called them to him and said to them, 'You know that those who are considered rulers of the Gentiles lord it over them, and their great ones exercise authority over them. But it shall not be so among you. But whoever would be great among you must be your servant,[a] and whoever would be first among you must be slave[b] of all. For even the Son of Man came not to be served but to serve, and to give his life as a ransom for many.'"

Great leaders are servants. The key question for us is, **"How can we live out servant leadership at home?"** Although I am writing on this topic, I admit I have such a long way to go in learning to prioritize leadership through service in my family relationships. Growing up I heard a lot about servant leadership, but I confess I find it easier to practice this outside of my home.

During my senior year, I was a part of a leadership team at Wheaton Academy called "Project Lead Discipleship." Our primary goal was to build relationships with underclassmen through service and community events. Every other week, our team would arrive two hours before school started to make a pancake breakfast for the underclassmen in order to further build relationships. This kind of service was easy for me! I was eager to engage at my school and sacrifice my own comfort (like an extra hour of sleep) to prioritize my ministry to my peers.

However, let's look at a similar situation in my home life. If my mom asks me to wake up an hour early to drive a sibling to school, or help make breakfast, I do not have that same eagerness to serve. My thoughts immediately jump to my own needs rather than the needs of my family.

Our homes are the hardest yet the most important places to practice servant leadership.

It's easy to serve when we want to, yet our homes are where our character is really tested, especially in regard to sibling relationships. With five younger siblings, it is super easy to fall into the habit of delegating jobs and responsibilities. For me, being a servant leader with my siblings requires that I do the job I don't want to do myself rather than delegating to a sibling. For teenagers with younger siblings, this message is for you! One of my biggest problems with my siblings is bossiness. I like to tell them what to do and expect them to do it. However, God has been convicting me that rather than telling my siblings what to do, I should first think of ways I can serve them. This often means doing the hardest job first.

While we could talk for a long time about how we can practice servant leadership at home, the truth is we are all at different spots in our life and our service to our families will look different. Here are some questions that I often ask myself to evaluate how I'm doing in regards to practicing servant leadership at home:

- When I am asked to do something, do I have a heart that is eager and happy to serve?

- Am I delegating work to my siblings or choosing to do it myself?

- Do I look for ways to serve my family without being told?

- Do I seek out opportunities in which I can serve and be a blessing to my family?

All of these questions may be difficult to face, but they will help us turn our hearts toward our families as we become servant leaders in our homes.

Scripture and Questions for Reflection/Discussion:

You, my brothers and sisters, were called to be free.
But do not use your freedom to indulge the flesh;
rather, serve one another humbly in love.

GALATIANS 5:13

Do nothing out of selfish ambition or vain conceit. Rather, in humility value others above yourselves, not looking to your own interests but each of you to the interests of the others.

PHILIPPIANS 2:3–4

1. How do these scriptures apply to your life at home with your family members?

2. What aspects of life around the house are you pushing off on others that you should be doing yourself? Pray for God to help you take action in those areas.

3. Do you see "selfish ambition" or "vain conceit" in your heart? In what ways? Have you confessed those things to God?

4. During this week ahead, what is one thing you can do to serve your family?